A1
Movers

Mini ^ Trainer

Two practice tests without answers

1

Cambridge University Press
www.cambridge.org/elt

Cambridge Assessment English
www.cambridgeenglish.org

Information on this title: www.cambridge.org/9781108585118

© Cambridge University Press and UCLES 2019

First published 2019

20 19 18 17

Printed in Poland by Opolgraf

A catalogue record for this publication is available from the British Library

ISBN 978-1-108-58511-8 Student's Book with Audio download

Acknowledgements

**The authors and publishers acknowledge the following sources of copyright material
and are grateful for the permissions granted. While every effort has been made, it has
not always been possible to identify the sources of all the material used, or to trace all
copyright holders. If any omissions are brought to our notice, we will be happy to include
the appropriate acknowledgements on reprinting and in the next update to the digital
edition, as applicable.**

The authors and publishers would like to thank the following contributors:

Page make up, illustration and animations: QBS Learning

Squirrel character illustration: Leo Trinidad

Cover illustration: Dan Widdowson

Author: Trish Burrow

Audio production: DN and AE Strauss Ltd and James Miller

Editor: Alexandra Miller

Contents

A1 Movers

Test 1   Training and Exam Practice

Test 2   Exam Practice

Vocabulary: Movers names

1 Listen to your teacher say the names and point.

Jane	Fred	Peter	Zoe	Paul
Clare	Jack	Charlie	Daisy	Vicky

Pre-Listening: describing people

2 Look at what the people are doing in Exercise 3. Say two things about the picture.

Listening for names and descriptions of people

3 002 Listen to a man and a girl talking about a picture. Point to the people they talk about. Then listen again and write the names.

_____ Fred _____   _____   _____

TIP! In the exam, look quickly at the picture while you listen to the example. Think of words you might hear to describe the people in the pictur

_____

TIP! Say what the people are doing, what they are wearing or what they look like.

Describing people

4 Test your partner! Cover your picture and describe the people.

Part 1
– 5 questions –

🔊 003 **Listen and draw lines. There is one example.**

Mary   Sam   Sally   Jim

Charlie   Lily   Clare

Vocabulary: spelling

1 `004` **Listen and write the words. Then say the word and spell it out loud.**

0 _swimsuit_

1 _____

2 _____

3 _____

4 _____

5 _____

6 _____

7 _____

8 _____

Vocabulary: numbers

2 `005` **Listen and point. Say the numbers. Then play *Bingo!***

35   72   63   44   13   89   96   52   28   67   38   41

TIP! Make sure that you write answers that make sense in Part 2.

Listening: listening for names, words and numbers

3 `006` **Look at the sentences. Then listen and write the answers.**

Visiting hospital

0	The family are visiting …	_Grandpa_ .
1	Fred wants to show photos of the …	_____ ride.
2	Grandpa hurt his …	_____ .
3	Grandpa is in room number …	_____ .
4	Fred wants to get some …	_____ for Grandpa.
5	Dinner time at the hospital is at …	_____ .

Part 2
– 5 questions –

 Listen and write. There is one example.

Homework

	Who is the homework for?	Mr _____ Best
1	Must write about:	A _____
2	Name of story:	My _____
3	Write homework in:	_____ book
4	Number of words:	_____
5	Day to give homework to teacher:	_____

Vocabulary: groups of words

1 What words do you know? Complete the word webs.

TIP! In Part 3, look at pictures A–H and think what words the pictures show before you listen.

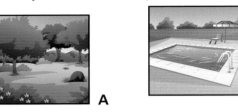
A

B

C

forest

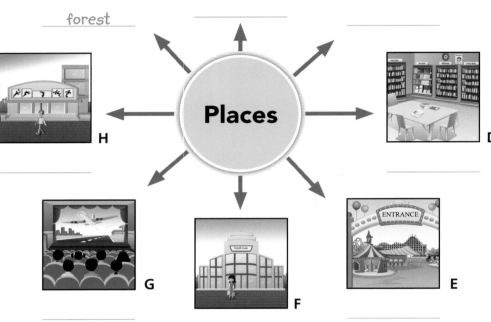

H

Places

D

G

F

E

A

B

C

H

Hobbies

D

G

F

E

TIP! Listen to all of the question before you write your tick.

Get ready!

2 [008] **Mr Snow is talking to Sarah about his family.**
What are the people in his family doing now? Listen and tick (✔).

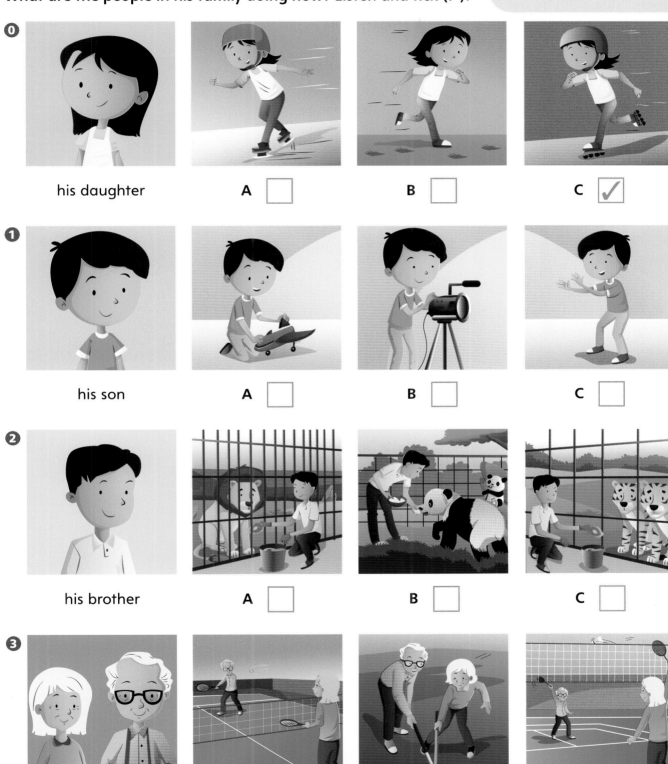

0   his daughter   A ☐   B ☐   C ✔

1   his son   A ☐   B ☐   C ☐

2   his brother   A ☐   B ☐   C ☐

3   his parents   A ☐   B ☐   C ☐

Part 3
– 5 questions –

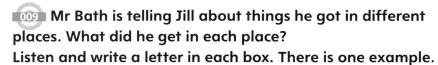

009 Mr Bath is telling Jill about things he got in different places. What did he get in each place?
Listen and write a letter in each box. There is one example.

the village [B]

the station ☐

the bus stop ☐

the car park ☐

the funfair ☐

the supermarket ☐

A

B

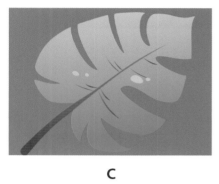

C

D

E

F

G

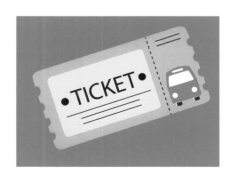

H

Pre-Listening: describing a picture

1 Look and say what you can see.

Listening for specific information

2 010 **Look at the pictures and describe them. Then listen and tick (✔) the box.**

> **TIP!** Listen to all of the conversation. Then choose the answer.

0 What does Clare want to eat?

A ☐   B ✔   C ☐

1 Which T-shirt is Nick looking for?

A ☐   B ☐   C ☐

2 What sport does Lily want to do at the sports centre?

A ☐   B ☐   C ☐

3 What is Kate doing?

A ☐   B ☐   C ☐

Part 4
– 5 questions –

 Listen and tick (✔) the box. There is one example.

Which film does Vicky want to watch?

A ✓   B ☐   C ☐

1 Who is Daisy's father?

A ☐   B ☐   C ☐

2 Where is Fred's brother now?

A ☐   B ☐   C ☐

3 What is Aunt Julia making?

A

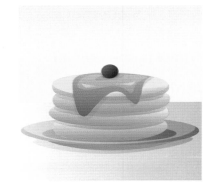

B

C

4 Where is the kitten now?

A

B

C

5 What is Dan doing?

A

B

C

Pre-Listening: listening carefully before you answer

1 Look at the posters (A–D) and say what you can see. Then listen and write a number in the box. Which poster are the people talking about?

 TIP! Look at the pictures before you listen. This helps you choose the correct answer.

A `0`
B ☐

C ☐
D ☐

Listening for specific information

2 Listen and colour and write. Colour four pictures and write one word.

 **TIP!** You hear the conversation two times. Remember to write one word and to colour four things in the picture.

Part 5
– 5 questions –

014 **Listen and colour and write. There is one example.**

Vocabulary: nouns

1 Put a circle around the word that is wrong.

0 Things you wear:	coat	(roof)	helmet	scarf
1 Places:	cinema	market	DVD	café
2 Food and drinks:	milkshake	bat	pasta	sandwich
3 People:	field	pop star	driver	farmer
4 Things in the home:	lamp	blanket	towel	sky

2 Look at the picture and write the words from Exercise 1 on the lines.

The Kangaroo Café

0 ___café___
1 _____
2 _____
3 _____
4 _____
5 _____

TIP! In Part 1, the answers are nouns like *kitten* or *swimsuit*. Learn the nouns on the Movers word list.

Grammar: verbs

3 Read the sentences. Then complete the sentences with words from the box.

TIP! In Part 1, the sentences have Starters and Movers verbs in them. Practice copying words carefully.

be   buy   cook   drive   ~~feed~~   go   ~~grow~~   is   like   moves   put   takes

0 Farmers _____grow_____ food in fields and some also
_____feed_____ their animals there.

1 Some people _____ upstairs and downstairs in a lift. It
sometimes _____ slowly.

2 A driver sometimes _____ you to school. They can
_____ a car, bus or train.

3 Some people _____ a blanket on their bed when it
_____ cold.

4 You can _____ fruit and vegetables in a market. Many
people _____ shopping there.

5 You must _____ careful when you _____
pasta because you use hot water.

17

Part 1
– 5 questions –

Look and read. Choose the correct words and write them on the lines. There is one example.

a dentist

a basement

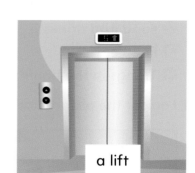
a lift

a supermarket

a driver

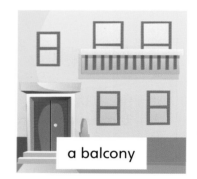
a balcony

a library

a doctor

Example

This person works in a hospital and helps people who are ill.   *a doctor*

Questions

❶ You can sit and read books in this place.   _____

❷ This takes people up or down to different floors in a building.   _____

❸ Go and see this person if your teeth hurt.   _____

❹ You can buy all kinds of food here.   _____

❺ This is part of a building that is under the ground.   _____

Responses to questions

1 Read the sentences. Then write the correct answer from the phrases in the box.

TIP! In Part 2, look at the questions and answers. Do they match and make sense?

> I love them.   It's opposite the bus station.   I've got some juice.
> Look, there are some in this comic.   ~~So do I!~~   That's a great
> idea! Yes, I went with my aunt.

0 I love playing tennis.   _So do I!_

1 Let's go to the park.   _____

2 Did you go to the cinema?   _____

3 Where is the new bookshop?   _____

4 Shall I get some drinks?   _____

5 Do you like noodles?   _____

6 I really like stories about aliens.   _____

Exam strategy: finding incorrect answers

2 Read the questions. Choose the correct answers. Say why the other answers are wrong.

0 What did you do at the weekend?   I played / ~~playing~~ / ~~play~~ football.

1 Who is your favourite pop star?   He plays the guitar. / Daisy Watson. / Their songs are great.

2 What's the matter, Mary?   She's got a cough. / He's sick today. / My foot hurts.

3 Where is your bag?   It's blue and white / in my bedroom / got my books in it.

4 When do you go swimming?   On Thursdays. / At the pool. / With my sister.

Your turn!

3 Read the conversations. Write a word in the gaps.

0 What did you do on Friday?

   a I _____went_____ to the sports centre.

   b I _played / bought_ computer games.

   c I _watched / saw_ a film on television.

1 How about buying a DVD for your brother?

   a What a nice _____!

   b He _____ love that.

   c Yes, he _____ watching films.

2 Which is your favourite story?

   a The story _____ pirates is good.

   b I like the pirate story _____.

   c Pirate stories _____ my favourite.

3 Let's go to the park this afternoon.

   a OK, we _____ play football.

   b _____ I bring my football?

   c Do you _____ to play football?

Part 2
– 6 questions –

Read the text and choose the best answer.

Example

Jack: What did you do yesterday, Vicky?

Vicky: A   I'm riding a horse.

                    B   I'm going riding.

                    C   I had a riding lesson.

Questions

1 Jack: Did you wear a helmet?

   Vicky: A   No, it isn't.

                   B   So do I.

                   C   Yes, I had to.

❷ Jack: Where did you ride?

   Vicky: A   After school.

                      B   Around the field.

                      C   At the weekend.

❸ Jack: Which horse did you ride?

   Vicky: A   It's called Mr Jim.

                      B   You would like it.

                      C   They were all grey.

❹ Jack: Who helped you?

   Vicky: A   Dad and my teacher.

                      B   Shall I help you?

                      C   We could do it.

❺ Jack: Was it easy to ride a horse?

   Vicky: A   No, I can't.

                      B   No, you weren't.

                      C   No, it wasn't.

❻ Jack: I'd love to ride a horse, too.

   Vicky: A   I went riding, too.

                      B   Well, come with me.

                      C   It's where I go.

Vocabulary: different kinds of words

1 Look at the words and write them in the correct group.

~~afraid~~ ~~blanket~~ bought carried coats **cold** dangerous
drive **field** forest frightened hospital ~~laughed~~
ride strongest travel warm **website**

Things	Actions	Adjectives
blanket	laughed	afraid

TIP! When you learn a new word, learn what kind of word it is and what words go before and after it.

Understanding the story first

2 Read the first two sentences of the story. What is it about? What do you think happens next?

Sally and Peter ride their bikes most weekends. Last Saturday it was very cold.

Now read all of the story. Were you right?

Sally and Peter ride their **bikes** most weekends. Last Saturday it was very **cold**. The children asked, 'Mum, can we go to the forest near the **lake** on our bikes?' Mum said, 'No, there is lots of ice on the roads — it's dangerous.' Dad said, 'Let's look on the internet and see what you can **do** today.' The family **looked** at the town website to find out something different to do. Peter said, 'Look! There's a new place on Island Road where we can go ice skating.' 'Let's go there!' said Sally. 'OK, get your coats, hats and **scarves**,' said Mum. 'You need to **wear** warm clothes for skating.' 'OK, Mum,' said the children. 'Shall we wear the sweaters Grandma and Grandpa bought us?' 'Yes, do that,' said Mum. 'And I can drive you to see them on the way home. They always love seeing you,' added Dad.

TIP! When you read a story, think what can happen next.

Now answer questions 1–5.

0 Where did Sally and Peter want to go? ___to the forest___

1 Why did their mum say they couldn't go out on their bikes? _____

2 Where did they look for ideas for something to do? _____

3 What do they choose to do? _____

4 What clothes did the children's mum say they should wear? _____

5 Who is Dad going to take the children to see? _____

Reading

3 Read the story again. Then write words from Exercise 2 below the pictures.

1 _____

2 _____

3 _____

4 _____

5 _____

6 _____

7 _____

8 _____

9 _____

4 Put the words in order to make possible names for the story. Then choose the best name for the story. Tick (✔) one box.

1 new / rides / Grandpa / bike / his _____ ☐

2 in / town / Ice / the / skating _____ ☐

3 the / lake / Ice / on _____ ☐

Part 3

– 6 questions –

**Read the story. Choose a word from the box. Write the
correct word next to numbers 1–5. There is one example.**

Peter loved going for long _____*walks*_____ with his father. Last week, they

went to a small lake.

'Can we swim here?' Peter asked.

'Sorry, Peter. The water's too **(1)** _____,' his father said.

There was a loud noise, which came from the **(2)** _____ opposite

the lake. 'What's that, Dad?' Peter asked.

'Is it a waterfall, Peter? It's very noisy,' Peter's father said.

'Yes, Dad! I think it is. Come on! Let's go and find it.' And they did!

Peter and his father **(3)** _____ on to the rocks, took off their boots

and socks and put their feet into the water. 'We can swim in this pool,' Peter's

father said. 'The water's great! And well done! You are the one who found

this brilliant place. Let's **(4)** _____ Mum a quick message.'

Peter smiled. 'OK. Let's have our **(5)** _____ here, too, Dad,' he said.

'Where are the sandwiches?'

Example

walks

text

thirsty

forest

headache

picnic

cold

climbed

top

(6) Now choose the best name for the story.

Tick one box.

Dad's funny message ☐

An exciting new place ☐

Peter swims in the lake ☐

Identifying the correct word

1 Read and choose the correct word to complete the sentences. What are the animals?

0 Some blue whales are longer (than) / **after** / **into** three buses!

1 They have strong legs **but** / **because** / **then** they can't run.

2 They are smaller **then** / **that** / **than** most whales and have small teeth.

3 There **is** / **are** / **was** 350 kinds of these birds in the world.

4 Some of these animals can **jumps** / **jump** / **jumping** between trees.

5 This animal **live** / **lives** / **living** in the jungle and can run and swim. It is orange and black.

Describing similarities and differences

2 Read the text and think what kind of word goes in the gaps. Then choose a word from the box. There are two extra words.

TIP! In Part 4, look at the words before and after the gaps to help you decide what the missing words are.

Lions come from Africa and are the second **(0)** _____biggest_____ cat in

the world. They are the only cats **(1)** _____ live in groups.

They live in groups of **(2)** _____ than ten lions, and

sometimes there are 40 of them! Lions eat other animals and they

often catch **(3)** _____ at night. They eat young elephants,

crocodiles and sometimes hippos. Lions like **(4)** _____ and

sleep for 16–20 hours a day on the ground or in a tree. Mother lions

have two or three baby lions, called 'cubs', and the other mother

lions **(5)** _____ to look after them.

biggest   help   more   sleeps   sleeping   that   them   then

Part 4
– 5 questions –

Read the text. Choose the right words and write them on the lines.

Bats

Example   Bats are small animals that live in different countries of the world. _____There_____

1   are hundreds of different kinds but _____ kind of bat can fly. Many bats

live in trees or roofs, but some live inside mountains. Most bats sleep in the day and

2   look for their food _____ night. Some bats eat fruit, but

3   _____ eat spiders and flies. Some bigger bats eat mice.

4   When bats _____ flying, they have to listen very carefully with their ears

5   because they don't see very _____ with their eyes.

Example	These	There	Them
1	both	every	this
2	into	near	at
3	another	everyone	lots
4	are	have	do
5	well	better	worse

Grammar: nouns, pronouns and possessive adjectives

1 Read the sentences and complete them with the words from the box.

> her   him   ~~It~~   it   their   them   They

0 Then the cow started to run after them. 'Look out! ____It____ is very fast!' said Daisy.

1 The family sat down by the river and had a picnic. _____ were very hungry after walking all morning.

2 Jim took his new camera to the beach. He took some fantastic photos with _____.

3 Dad told _____ to take their helmets with them.

4 The children didn't do _____ homework so the teacher wasn't very happy.

5 'Where is your grandpa? I can't see _____ in the field,' asked Grandma.

6 Sue looked for _____ tablet, then she found it in the dog's bed.

TIP! In this part, learn to recognise which words are referred to when we use pronouns and possessive adjectives.

Exam strategy: say the same thing in a different way

2 Read the sentences from different stories. Colour the words in them that you can use to complete the second sentences. Then write in the gaps.

0 On Friday the family ate breakfast in the garden.
The family had breakfast in the garden ____on Friday____.

1 Last week, Sam's dad said, 'Let's go to the new shopping centre. I would like to buy a new coffee machine.'
Sam's dad wanted to buy a new _____ at the shopping centre.

2 It snowed a lot on Thursday, so Bill's school was closed.
Bill couldn't go to _____ on Thursday, because it snowed a lot.

3 'I'd like to make meatballs for dinner, but we haven't got any meat!' said Vicky's mum.
Vicky's mother needed to buy _____ to make dinner that day.

4 'I know a very good website where we can buy some new shoes,' said Fred.
Fred knew a _____ where you could buy new shoes.

5 'Thanks, Mum and Dad,' said Matt. 'My birthday party was brilliant.'
Matt thanked his parents for a _____ birthday party.

TIP! In Part 5, the words you use to complete the sentences are always in the story and you copy 1, 2 or 3 words.

Get ready!

**3 Look at the pictures. What do you think happens in the story?
Read the story and answer the questions.**

Zoe's family lived in an apartment in the city centre, but in the school holidays she went to see her grandparents on their farm in the countryside. Last Saturday, Zoe's parents drove her there. Zoe was very happy. 'I'd like to feed the baby goats! When she texted me last week, Grandma told me there are ten of them this year!'

Examples

Where was Zoe's apartment?   in the city centre
Where did Zoe go in the school holidays?
her grandparents' farm

Questions

❶ How did Zoe's grandma tell her there were lots of baby animals this year? _____

❷ What was Zoe happy about feeding? _____

They were surprised when they got to the farm and saw there was nothing in the garden where Zoe's grandparents grew carrots and peas. 'Some animals ate all the vegetables!' said Zoe's grandma, 'I can't make vegetable soup for you, like I always do. There were lots of vegetables in our garden last week and we can't find the animals that ate them.' 'Well, I want to know which animals ate all the vegetables!' said Zoe.

❸ What wasn't in the garden when Zoe's family got to the farm? _____

❹ What did Grandma always make for Zoe's family? _____

❺ What did Zoe say she wanted to know? _____

Zoe found an old cage in one of the farm buildings and she put it in the garden. 'I think it's a hungry goat that is eating all the carrots and peas. Goats like vegetables,' thought Zoe, so she asked her grandpa to give her some salad leaves and she put them in the cage. That night Zoe dreamed about a huge goat that was eating all the vegetables and the flowers, too! In the morning, Zoe's grandma said, 'Zoe, come quickly! I know what was eating all our food now.' And she showed Zoe a family of rabbits. 'What naughty rabbits!' said Zoe.

❻ What did Zoe put in the cage, so that she could catch the animals that were eating the vegetables? _____

Part 5
– 7 questions –

Look at the pictures and read the story. Write some words to complete the sentences about the story. You can use 1, 2 or 3 words.

Lily's busy morning

Lily really enjoyed learning and loved school. Last Thursday evening she carefully chose the things she needed for all of her lessons and took her school clothes out of the cupboard and put them on her chair.

On Friday morning, Lily woke up at six o'clock. She went quietly to the bathroom and had a shower. Then she put on her school shirt and skirt and went downstairs to make her breakfast. She liked doing that. She found some bread and grapes and made some hot chocolate to drink.

Examples

On ___Thursday___ evening Lily found everything she needed for school.

Lily woke up at six o'clock on _Friday morning_ .

Questions

❶ After her _____, Lily got dressed and went downstairs.

❷ For her breakfast, Lily ate some _____ and drank some hot chocolate.

Lily put her books and pens and pencils in her bag at seven o'clock and then washed her cup and plate. Then she gave the cat its food. Then she read the answers to some homework questions carefully. There were no mistakes! Then she read about her favourite animals, polar bears, on her father's laptop.

At eight o'clock, her parents came downstairs. They were surprised. Lily had her school clothes on.

❸ Lily fed the _____ .

❹ Lily looked at the _____ to some questions and read about some polar bears.

❺ When Lily's parents saw their daughter in her school clothes, they were _____ .

'There's no school today!' her father said.

Lily's mother quickly had an idea. 'We can go to the library this morning. You can learn lots of

new things there!' she said.

Lily smiled. Mum was right.

6 _____ had a good idea!

7 Lily was happy. She could learn a hundred new things at the _____.

Vocabulary

1 Put a tick (✔) if you can see or a cross (✘) if you can't see the things in the picture.

clouds ☐	moon ☐	monkeys ☐	tree ☐
ship ☐	jellyfish ☐	parrots ☐	girl ☐
boy ☐	bottle ☐	man ☐	woman ☐
bowl ☐	helicopter ☐	rainbow ☐	

TIP! In Part 6, think of questions about the picture and how to answer them.

Answering questions about a picture

2 Match the questions and answers.

> A bottle with a message in it.
> She's climbing a tree.
> A man and a woman.
> ~~They are by a waterfall.~~

> It's jumping out of the water.
> A helicopter and some clouds.
> He's taking a photo.

0 Where are the people and animals?   _They are by a waterfall._

1 What can you see in the sky?   _____

2 What is the fish doing?   _____

3 Who is in the boat?   _____

4 What is the man trying to catch?   _____

5 What is the boy doing?   _____

6 What is the girl doing?   _____

Your turn!

3 Look at the picture and the mixed up words. Make sentences about the picture.

TIP! Think carefully about the order of the words. In Part 6 you write two complete sentences about the picture.

Example

garden / day / It's / sunny / the / a / in

It's a sunny day in the garden.

❶ man / and / lemonade / woman / drinking / The / are

_____

❷ baby / drawing / The / is / the / girl

_____

❸ table / a / on / There's / book / the

_____

❹ game / children / are / football / a / of / Two / playing

_____

❺ swimming / with / in / pool / girls / ball / are / The / playing / a / the

_____

Part 6
– 6 questions –

Look and read and write.

Examples

What are the chickens doing?　　　　　eating

Who is driving the tractor?　　　　　the woman

Complete the sentences.

❶ Two of the buildings have got a round _____.

❷ The boy is wearing a pair of _____.

Answer the questions.

❸ Where are the rabbits? _____

❹ Which animal is crossing the river? _____

Now write two sentences about the picture.

❺ _____

❻ _____

Describing differences

1 Look at the two pictures. Put a circle around the four differences.
Then in pairs write sentences. Take turns to describe the differences.

Picture 1

Picture 2

0 Here the girl has got _____*blue*_____ skates.

1 _____

2 _____

3 _____

4 _____

0 Here the girl has got _____*red*_____ skates.

1 _____

2 _____

3 _____

4 _____

TIP! In this part of the test the differences are often colours, size, number, position or activities.

Further practice

2 Look at picture 1. Draw five differences in picture 2 and colour it. In pairs, describe your picture and draw your partner's picture in your notebook.

Find the differences

Answering support questions

1 Look at the pictures and answer the questions.

Mary goes to the funfair

Mary

Mary and her dad are at home. Mary is saying, 'Can we go to the funfair, Dad? Mary's father is saying 'Yes, we can go this afternoon.'

Where are Mary and her father?
What ride does Mary want to go on?
How many people are waiting to go on the ride?

Where are they now?
Is Mary enjoying the ride?
What about her father?

Who wants to go on the ride again?
How does Mary's father feel?
What is Mary saying?
What is Mary's father saying?

Telling a coherent story

2 Look at the pictures and put them in order 1–4.

The monkeys help Jim

 a

 b

 c

d

Jim

TIP! Think of questions about the pictures to help you talk about them. In the exam, you don't see the questions.

TIP! In the exam, first look at all the pictures quickly to try to understand the story. Then say one or two sentences about each picture.

Part 2

Paul's friends come to help!

Paul

Categorising vocabulary

1 Look and say the words. Then write them in the table.

Computers	Parts of the body	Sea animals	Clothes	Places
laptop				

TIP! When learning new words or revising vocabulary put words in groups that are the same.

Describing similarities and differences

2 Look at the pictures and complete the sentences.

0    **1**

2   **3**

0 The coat, the sweater and the swimsuit are all _____red_____ and the scarf is _____blue_____.

1 These animals are all _____ and the _____ is _____.

2 These places are all _____ and the _____ is _____.

3 You play _____ with these things and you watch a _____ with this thing.

TIP! You only have to give simple reasons for the different picture.

Odd one out

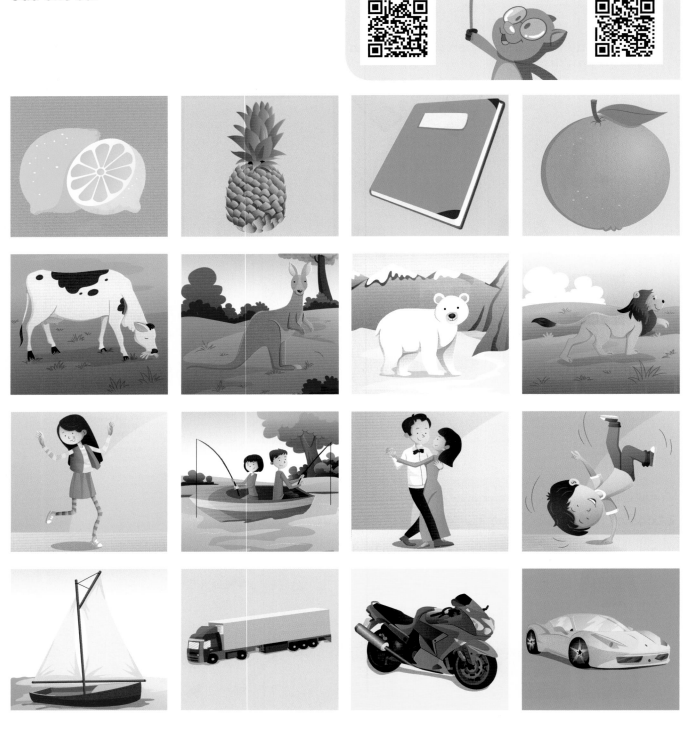

Part 4

Tell me something about your classroom.

Part 1

– 5 questions –

015 **Listen and draw lines. There is one example.**

Lily   Fred   Vicky   Zoe

Jim   Paul   Julia

Part 2

– 5 questions –

 Listen and write. There is one example.

Going to a friend's house

Example

Who going to see   _____Mary_____ Point

Questions

1 | Where friend lives: in _____ Tree Road

2 | Which day to go there: on _____

3 | When to go there: at _____ o'clock

4 | What to do there: _____

5 | How to travel there: by _____

Part 3
– 5 questions –

017 Mrs Grace is telling Peter about her birthday presents. What did each person give to Mrs Grace? Listen and write a letter in each box. There is one example.

her grandson   E

her uncle

her cousin

her daughter

her granddaughter

her son

A

B

C

D

E

F

G

H

Part 4
– 5 questions –

 Listen and tick (✔) the box. There is one example.

Which sport is Charlie learning to play now?

A ☐

B ☐

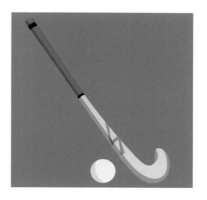

C ✓

1 What does Dad want Jane to do?

A ☐

B ☐

C ☐

2 Where is Jack's red sweater now?

A ☐

B ☐

C ☐

3 Which friend is called Clare?

A ☐

B ☐

C ☐

4 Which website is Mum looking at?

A ☐

B ☐

C ☐

5 What is the baby doing now?

A ☐

B ☐

C ☐

Part 5
– 5 questions –

019 Listen and colour and write. There is one example.

Part 1
– 5 questions –

Look and read. Choose the correct words and write them on the lines.
There is one example.

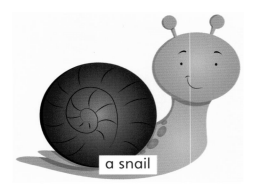

a snail

tea

cheese

a parrot

a picnic

a shark

a lion

vegetables

Example

Onions, beans and peas are examples of these.   _vegetables_

Questions

1 This can fly and some of them can talk.   _____

2 People make this from milk. You can put it in sandwiches.   _____

3 This has a large shell on its back and moves very slowly.   _____

4 Some people put lemon in this drink.   _____

5 This lives in the sea and some people are afraid of it.   _____

Part 2
– 6 questions –

Read the text and choose the best answer.

Example

Mary:	Do you like playing the piano, Dan?

Dan:	Ⓐ Yes, very much.
	B Yes, please.
	C Yes, I can.

Questions

❶ Mary: When do you practise?

Dan: A   Last Tuesday.

                     B   Yes, I have to.

                     C   After school.

2 Mary: Where is your piano?

Dan: A   That isn't right.

                   B   In the living room.

                   C   It's on the top.

3 Mary: Is it very difficult to play the piano?

Dan: A   Yes, but I enjoy it.

                   B   Yes, it's easy.

                   C   Yes, I'm playing it.

4 Mary: What kind of music is your favourite?

Dan: A   I like music.

                   B   I like it best.

                   C   I like everything.

5 Mary: How about playing something for me?

Dan: A   OK, come with me.

                   B   I'm fine, thank you.

                   C   Yes, it was brilliant.

6 Mary: I want to learn to play the guitar.

Dan: A   You can tell me.

                   B   So do I!

                   C   It's not mine.

Part 3
– 6 questions –

Read the story. Choose a word from the box. Write the correct word next to numbers 1–5. There is one example.

Lucy enjoyed reading stories to her _____little_____ brother, Hugo. His favourite

was about an old man who **(1)** _____ a clever monkey in the jungle to

make banana cakes! The old man had a long beard and funny moustache. Last

Saturday, Hugo said, 'Why can't I have a beard and moustache, Lucy?'

'Because only men can grow those.'

Hugo was **(2)** _____ when his big sister said that.

On Sunday, Lucy found her paint box. 'I've got a great **(3)** _____,

Hugo,' she said.

Lucy carefully painted a black moustache and a beard on her brother's face.

When she was happy with her work, Hugo looked at his face in the

(4) _____ in the bathroom.

'Wow!' he said. 'I love my moustache and beard, but I can never clean my

face again.'

'Don't **(5)** _____ your face now, Hugo,' Lucy said. 'But you must do

that before you go to bed. Sorry!'

Example

little	mirror	build
idea	sad	world
taught	sunny	wash

(6) Now choose the best name for the story.

Tick one box

Hugo writes a story   ☐

Lucy helps her brother   ☐

An old man finds a monkey   ☐

Part 4
– 5 questions –

Read the text. Choose the right words and write them on the lines.

Kangaroos

Example
Kangaroos sometimes get very hungry because they live _____in_____ countries where the weather is often very hot and dry. The grass and small plants

1 that kangaroos eat don't grow well when there isn't _____ rain!

2 Kangaroos have two huge feet and two of _____ legs are long and strong. They can hop very quickly on these two legs. But kangaroos can't move

3 quickly when they walk _____ all four legs. Kangaroos have strong

4 tails, which help them to _____. Did you know that kangaroos can

5 swim too? _____ are four kinds of kangaroo and most live in Australia.

Example	in	by	with
1	many	any	lots
2	they	them	their
3	up	on	off
4	jump	jumps	jumping
5	Those	Another	There

Part 5
– 7 questions –

Look at the pictures and read the story. Write some words to complete the sentences about the story. You can use 1, 2 or 3 words.

Who takes the best photos?

Nick and his older cousin, Alice, both enjoyed taking photos of different people. Nick took his with his camera. Alice took hers with her phone.

Last Monday, they went to the new shopping centre with Alice's parents to buy some new clothes. In their favourite shop they saw May Night, a famous pop star! It was very exciting to see her and Nick and Alice wanted to take some photos of her.

Examples

Alice was _____ older _____ than her cousin, Nick.

One of their hobbies was taking photos _of different people_ .

Questions

❶ Last Monday, Alice's parents took Alice and Nick to the new _____ .

❷ The children saw a _____ called May Night in a clothes shop.

May laughed and said, 'OK!' when they asked her to stand and smile in different parts of the store.

When they got back home, Nick and Alice looked at their photos on Alice's laptop.

'Mine are fantastic!' said Alice.

'Yes, but mine are better than yours!' said Nick.

❸ Alice and Nick took photos of May in _____ of the shop.

❹ The children looked at the pictures on _____ when they got home.

❺ Nick thought his photos were _____ Alice's!

Alice sent all their photos to a pop music comic that they both read every week. Nick was really happy when he saw three of his photos and three of Alice's photos in the comic! He sent a text to Alice which said, 'I showed our photos to all of my friends in school this morning. I think we BOTH take fantastic photos!'

'Me too!' Alice said. 'Hooray! Well done, Nick, and well done me!'

6 Nick saw the photos of May in the _____ .

7 Nick was really happy and texted _____ to say all the photos were fantastic.

Part 6

– 6 questions –

Look and read and write.

Examples

How many islands are there? _____two_____

What's the weather like? ___sunny and windy___

Complete the sentences.

1 There is some _____ in an old box under the sea.

2 The dolphins are grey, pink and _____ .

Answer the questions.

3 Where are the three shells? _____

4 Who is jumping into the sea? _____

Now write two sentences about the picture.

5 _____

6 _____

Find the differences

Learning about trees!

Nick

Odd one out